canvas

poems

james c. morehead

Viewless Wings
Press

Copyright © 2021 by James Christopher Morehead
All rights reserved.
Published in the United States by Viewless Wings Press, Dublin, California.
Library of Congress Control Number: 2021904280
Hardcover ISBN 978-1-7367890-3-2 | Paperback ISBN 978-1-7367890-0-1
Ebook ISBN 978-1-7367890-1-8
viewlesswingspress.com

10 9 8 7 6 5 4 3 2 1

First Edition

Cover art: Kari Byron
Interior art: Kari Byron (*midnight wanderer, mawu after midnight, wade, reach, powder*)
and Alla Tsank (*falling, beauty*)
Photographs: James Morehead (*by the ocean, stages, in the city. ricochets, limano, five towers, arcata community forest, ode to sabby, music for an abandoned warehouse*)
and Kari Byron (*carved*)
Cover and book design: Zoe Norvell
Editing: Mary Morehead and Philip Morehead
Copy Editing: Brittany Smail

canvas

Contents

Author's Note

I was introduced to writing poetry by a creative writing teacher in high school. I had always enjoyed writing (and was a shy, voracious bookworm) but hadn't experimented with poetry. I had the typical high school student's impression of poetry: boring, hard to understand, and worst of all nerdy. But that teacher was the spark, and during the section on poetic forms I discovered the extraordinary power of poetry: the ability to capture emotion, sound, and movement in a few carefully crafted words. Reading E.E. Cummings, more than any other poet, taught me the design language of poetry.

Over the past forty years I've had bursts of creativity and long lulls of blank pages, but always lurking was a need to capture my experiences in words. The year 2020 and its pandemic-induced solitude inspired the poems of which I'm most proud; they lead this collection. Most are autobiographical, in particular the title poem "canvas," and collectively form a fragmented memoir of memories and melancholy. Some are fanciful, like "tethered," inspired by a fleeting image seen while hiking the Pacific coastline. All strive to paint images in the reader's mind through the thoughtful selection and careful placement of words.

For Mary, Emily, and Evelyn

one

heart racing from stress dreams:
fleeing or falling or any of the frenetic scenes
that purge my mind of pandemic news
only to be refilled day after day after quarantine day

canvas

i stretch myself over the frame pulled taut to smooth skin's creases my
canvas set awaiting your first stroke

you lay out the brushes with care bristles clean and dry

    the first brush its head cut sharp to detail the subtle wrinkles around my eyes

    the second wide to fill my laughing smile

    the third rough to capture a storm swelling behind me over the sea

    and one more a piercing point to drop a tear that belies my melancholy

stepping back you scan me before preparing your palette

what shade of caucasian to choose for my sun-aged skin? how much grey
will you need to sneak silver threads into my thick brown hair? how
should you dress me? what textures will you drape? am i alone on a trail or
seething in a concert crowd? how will you capture the chaotic cacophony
swirling in my mind with only strokes of oil?

and how can you reflect everything i've seen into the detail of my eyes
and are they wide open alert unable to find sleep or quivering and fighting
exhaustion or are they shut tight and twitching in rem-triggered dreams or
are they still serene like death?

i think you should start with my memories so many to choose from you
can't possibly paint them all lest the layers grow so deep that the color slides
from me dripping forgotten onto the floor

perhaps start with the bliss of running through a new england park pulling a kite its fluttering tail flying up into the crisp fall breeze the kritch kritch sound of leaves beneath my feet

perhaps start with the melancholy of bullies fear that started in sixth grade and lingered relentless until my scrawny frame sprouted six feet tall in high school

perhaps start with the sound of music from my parents' practicing while i lie beneath the steinway floating on waves of notes as father's fingers race the keys while mother's oboe pierces the chords

or perhaps start with the near silence of when i escape the frenetic digital pulse and head onto a trail stepping in rhythm until hours later i lie back eyes closed to let my ears explore the forest depths

i hope you choose to paint me with my eyes wide open so i can see your expression as you apply the final stroke

and when you are done and the paint is drying its pungent odor slowly fading and imperceptible until the last molecule of scent escapes

and when you walk away your brushes cleaned and neatly packed your tubes of paint capped and stored

will you remember me? will you remember each brush stroke and shade of oil? will you be relieved to finish me to escape this dreary task or will you wait until the palette runs dry so we can share this moment a little longer?

by the ocean

awoken again reaching out in darkness

heart racing from stress dreams: fleeing or falling or any of the frenetic scenes that purge my mind of pandemic news only to be refilled day after day after quarantine day

fingers fumbling to find the hour knowing it will be the quiet time when you can stretch your ears for miles only to find more silence and the occasional whistle of wind

staring into the black i try unsuccessfully the tricks of sleep counting sheep and rhythmic breathing until i think of you: standing by the ocean buffeted by a stiff eastward salt-scented breeze kerchief-sheltered from the crispness

"sometimes you have to just turn off the news" you say "and listen to nothing" (the distinct voice of rippling waves whispering behind you)

i let loose of the swirling thoughts that race my heart and exhaust my mind and imagine your voice and the crashing waves and stepping out under a new moon onto sand slipping off my shoes and socks to feel my way across the beach

i let the darkness wrap around me between the moonless sky and blue-black water holding me tight and soaking up the still swirling thoughts until sky sea and stillness take me away

the stress dreams are silenced for now sleep taking hold and insomniac rustling subsided slipping back into darkness until their inevitable return

routine

alarm sounding shuffling of sheets tip-toe barefoot to the bathroom sink
flossing brushing then with the same spoon rinsed and overnight dried in
a yellowed dish tray scoop up cheerios in clumps milk drops dripping one
by one until a single o remains bobbing aimlessly

the drive to work by rote over tire-streaked freeway overpasses and carpool
lanes and timing the exit merge and racing a yellow light until tucking into
the same parking lot cubby as yesterday the day before and the day before

car door clicks trunk swooshes open backpack fetched footsteps tracing
a well-worn shortcut across the campus lawn avoiding a cyclist's spinning
and for a moment looking up because i always do this time of year when
california sunshine burns through morning fog

my desk untouched yesterday's coffee mug hydrating flask computer power
cord dangling books i may someday read family photos framed rest quietly
staring back at me day after day until i box them up for another office
cubicle or leave them behind forgotten

good morning i say good morning they say day after day with smiles
sometimes genuine sometimes forced sometimes masking unbearable sadness
resentment boredom intrigue until formalities finished i disappear into earbuds
and shuffled playlists or pretend listening to discourage chatty cubemates

it's likely at lunch that i'll walk down the same aisle and select the same
plate and linger but settle for the same entrée selection as yesterday and
sit silent in my favorite corner nook peering out across the bay through
window-washer-streaked panes

and leaving work i'll retrace each off-ramp lane change shortcut and
eventually close my eyes and dreamlike in a podcast-fueled autopilot turn
into the cul-de-sac garage door squeaking sliver of light peeking and a smile
in the doorway welcoming me home

i fall into sleep and randomly dream until morning sun wakes to shelter-
in-place and we're told to stay home by a broadcast email and toilet paper is
suddenly rare oh how much i long for my old routine that can only return if
they find a vaccine

now

i remember vacation planning
the sound of clicking in search of a deal
dk travel guides bookmarked with post-its
and a countdown pinned to my wall

i remember ticketmaster scrambles at 10am
refreshing the page to secure a coveted row
blocking my calendar and counting the days
until lights out: the band takes the stage

i remember couples scheduling weddings
baseball fans who stubhub tickets
i remember graduates groomed for commencement
and parents strategizing for good seats

but life has become now and not when
planning suspended our futures opaque
days looped together in time escher folds
forced to live in the moment whatever it holds

stages

1

a snap brings darkness and the crowd comes to life
packed tight in waves that rush towards the stage
while flashlight beams guide the bandmates through space
over cables taped snug past speakers humming bright

each stage a glowing wall of sound
plumes of smoke pouring into the pit
and floating up to refract laser trails
while vari-lites dance to a pulsing beat

robert smith hair teased a moody mop
trent reznor synthesizer keys sent scattering
siouxie's banshees layered curtains revealed
prince preening purple cabaret voltaire abstract green

at the fillmore escape from the stage heading upstairs
past walls papered with psychedelic posters swirling colors
dylan grateful stones hendrix each sold-out show preserved
the balcony walls glowing from chandeliers' crystals

2

down by market marquees shine bright
nestled between elegant italian and bustling thai
buzz and anticipation flow past the will call line
finding aisle row seat until the theatre lights dim

this audience is silent ears perked and waiting
stage left a figure appears from the shadows
"now is the winter of our discontent" he bellows
glorious held in a tracking beam of light

3

three thousand miles east broadway stages are set and dressed
a couple steps onto the curb and through lyceum's doors
settling into jacket-draped seats hands fiddling playbill pages
until the curtain reveals colorful performers in choreographed song

4

in a northern canadian cathedral a simpler stage is set
beneath a vaulted steeple and its rich acoustic echo
a man caresses a piano a woman teases an oboe
their audience nestled row on row in silent solitude

5

but now the stages are empty and dark
their performers all sheltered in place
uncertain when the spotlights return
their soliloquy songs suspended in space

today?

first I think it's monday from my quarantined confines
i look outside for any clues to offer me a sign

then again it could be tuesday when deliveries come
the fedex truck will drop surprises boxed and on the run

perhaps it's wednesday when a corgi strolls by with a prance
she (or he?) might briefly pause so i can catch a glance

when thursday comes grocery bags the welcome mat does fill
but my fridge is packed so neatly stacked it can't be thursday still

if friday's here then weekend's near but hard to know for sure
will they ever vaccinate to make a time-loop cure?

wait yesterday was saturday! i watched my favorite show!
but perhaps I watched a replay I recorded days ago?

i expect a call on wednesday so if my phone is buzzing
i'll have a clue mystery solved get right back to my gardening...

...that thing i do each thursday morn to fill the passing hours
i tend each planter lovingly awaiting springtime flowers

but then i notice silence as i wander down the hall
the air so still it must be sunday heading into fall

perhaps the days have lost all meaning to infinity
an escher looped back on itself to circle ceaselessly

pieces

we've taken over the dining room table its white plastic protector perfect
for sliding silhouetted pieces into place 1000 image fragments dumped out
between us in a jumble of curlicued edges

i balance the box lid on edge to be our guide: a photographed row of
colorful townhouses lining a canal that reminds me of san francisco's
painted ladies

you chose this puzzle with infinite blue claiming you see subtle differences
in the shades of sky; my aging eyes see only sameness

(you've always been a puzzle lover – or is it puzzler or puzzlist? – a new box
appearing each christmas under the tree; later warmed by a crackling fire
we crowd around the table with my mother taking the lead)

we start by finding edges to corral the pieces and prevent them sneaking back
into the box or falling lost forever beneath a cupboard burrowed in dust

next we divide and conquer: i build the row of townhouses while you tackle
that infinite blue each piece connected triggering a dose of pleasure fueling
the search for another hit

for every piece i place you place ten and i marvel at your skill mapping the
image in your mind while effortlessly untangling the jumbled stacks of color

at some point you'll remark *what's the point of puzzles anyway why chop up an
image just to put it back together again* we'll leave the question hanging like we
do every year

inevitably visitors stop by *oh wow look how much you've done* some will offer
a helping hand connecting a piece or two before quietly slipping away

searching for pieces i imagine strolling along the canal memorizing each
detail as i go pausing by the shuttered windows and for a time transported

(perhaps couples should complete a puzzle of their partner's image to
rediscover subtle details forgotten years ago)

as we cross midnight our eyes watering i wonder who lives inside these
colorful townhouses? who sails the boats anchored in the canal outside?
were they sleeping when the photo was taken? or waking awaiting
breakfast? or perhaps trapped behind the shutters suspended in time?

in the silence of early morning after hours of *just one more piece* only
one piece remains; without fanfare you complete the puzzle and calmly
announce *dad let's start the next one*

two

and now each fall passing and cycle of leaves
autumns behind me stacked higher than waiting ahead
i cling to each breath of crisp scented breeze
and try not to blink looking out over the trees

falling

with a damp chill and shortening days
i drive past dorset at autumn's peak
high above white clouds stroll puffed in promenade
held delicate together by slender contrails
and morning sun softly warms a crisp early breeze
sending lake shimmered ripples a cumulus mirror

i step into a forest maples rooted firm in canadian shield
feet meandering in search of a tickling leaf crunch
all the while drinking air soaked yellow orange red brown
in time the breeze grows unsettled around
a bluster that rips determined leaves from their perches
scattering like startled butterflies a colorful stochastic flutter

i walk alone thankful threatening nimbus halts its advance
and slip through the leaves past seasons years decades
transported from canada to a new england vista
passing through time and space into a 70s country wagon
where the roads ever curving slide me across the trunk floor
as we slip on to gravel in search of a fall fair

touching a pumpkin's husk hurls me again into space
to boston's freedom trail outside faneuil's hall
with autumn colors draping the worn graves of patriots
and the tickling crunch unchanged despite decades passing
through boston common king's chapel down ever-twisting walkways
where artists balance canvases and sketch with fingerless gloves

in a moment falling again through the city to rural vermont
winding through postcard towns and white painted gazebos
nestled still in rust-draped appalachians
i step into waterbury hugged warm in a peacoat
strolling down uneven sidewalks past sleeping storefronts
to stir and crunch leaves from their wind-structured stacks

finally falling surrounded the sweet scent of decay
burrowing deep into earth past shadow seeking light
until mildew and grey give way to newton's morning
sunshine bright sparkling through orange-tinged edges
leaping out of the pile a burst of oak and elm
distant memories of youth when time had no meaning

and now each fall passing and cycle of leaves
autumns behind me stacked higher than waiting ahead
i cling to each breath of crisp scented breeze
and try not to blink looking out over the trees
and listen to each crunch as i step through the leaves
until i catch a fell maple to welcome me home

crush

teen week at foxwood inn
i'm fifteen scrawny bookwormed and shy
she arrives so tall her rich brown curls waving
a smile dazzling and confident

the crush envelopes me
its weight taking my breath away
as she turns the corner there is no time to say hi
and i fear being caught staring too long

each morning after breakfast
i peek over my paperback
waiting for her to pass by and if her eyes catch mine
i shrink and blush my heart crushed and racing

later by the dock
the jocks show off their running shirtless headlong dives
while i sit silently on a fading muskoka chair
tucking my book under a towel avoiding splashes

when the last night comes her name a mystery still
with stairway to heaven's sorrowful intro begun
i crush fear walking towards her
extending my hand offering a dance

she looks me in the eye
and quietly nods no
and takes the dance floor with one of the diving boys

i walk into darkness across dew–damp grass
down to the end of the dock
sitting legs swinging toes caressing the still cool lake
robert plant echoing in the distance

between chords i hear footsteps
she's there her hand on my shoulder
a tear sliding down my cheek
"i like you james but just as a friend"
sitting down beside me as the song ends

i feel the crush as my imagined first kiss
drifts away with the ripples beneath my feet
but in time smile eyes closed and dry
replaying her saying my name

shadow's play

the shadow enters on cue
behind viewers row on row
hands set shoulders still
following players' spotlit forms
and well-worn phrases
projected over the darkened theater

the shadow floats unseen
between a couple's hands entwined
a child tugging with whispered questions
and a solitary critic quietly scribbling

the shadow slips delicately along the stage
invisible to the spotlight's tracking beam
and illuminated twinkles of drifting dust

but the stage manager suspicious is watchful
from a booth tucked high above
adjusts her squinting glasses
searching
while the apparition plays tricks
in the orchestra pit

the shadow sensing drifts stage right
tucks behind a gilded throne adorned with
plastic jewels casting deceptive sparkles
no more real than a silhouette's touch

and with that the shadow melts into the stage
among the words and phrases
masquerade and dancers
foiled fighters' tears
and fools' laughter
her voice long since hidden and forgotten
her steps no longer beholden to blocking
her beating heart just a trick of light
that vanishes in curtained darkness

sisters

two sisters twirl to a mandolin round
their fresh golden daisies sewn into braids
and eyes that sparkle by autumn's bright fire
flicker with laughter as embers take flight

two sisters with play swords carved out of pine
parry and thrust on scaligera's wall
peeking through splays before bursting forward
race to the turret flying past newels

far below castle walls lake garda wakes
its smooth mirrored surface shivers in waves
a daisy flies free from emily's hair
her sister gives chase to battlement's edge

each holding their swords they scurry below
passageways flickering candlelight glow
over the drawbridge suspended in place
flashes of anger burst out of the sky

two sisters run to the fog-shrouded shore
their swords and their shields unraveling braids
melting like sandcastles into high tide
ripples of laughter from where they now hide

midnight wanderer

the midnight wanderer glides through darkness

home from work working late
wandering silent in multispectral gadgets' glow
red white green pinpoints of light leading down the hall
one by one by one tentative feeling footfalls
testing for the top step pausing by the landing's turn
white noise patter from the fountain outside
floating in steady hypnotic patterns
clutch lurch whirr as the furnace awakes

camouflaged by fountain and furnace
feeling the way in deepening darkness
fingers follow the wall
footstep's path traced in memory
sleeping daughters surrounded by dreams' ebb and flow
blow a midnight kiss
then back down the hall to pause in moon's crest
creeping out from behind shifting clouds
then gone

pupils black and wide to steal light in darkness
shadows whisper
dresser to the left nightstand to the right
slide into sheets under covers
nestle sideways breath held tight
sense her breathing rise and fall
eyes close shadows stolen blackness total

                                        out

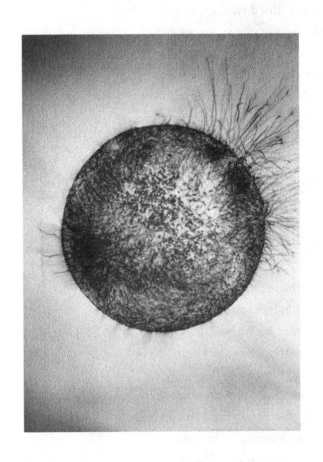

gale in suburbia

pacific born the midnight gale arrives
a whistling force in darkness howling cry
unsettled gusts that drive me wide awake
i search for sleep in vain as shutters shake

backyard umbrellas rattle in their stands
and soon they're freed as fury lifts them up
when flying fails they crash back to the ground
(i wonder who's awoken by the sound)

our chimney starts to hum a single tone
a booming note with angry ebbs and flows
the neighbor's chimney calls out to reply
a windy chorus singing to the sky

p g and e is shutting power off
across the court lights go out with a snap
neighbors wake in pitch black wondering why
peek through the curtains looking to the sky

trees flung upended lie across the street
their freshly planted roots could not hold firm
a passing high beam lights the slivered bark
distracted drivers glance into the dark

in time the wind subsides and calm returns
suburbia's no longer in distress
interrupted dreams resume their courses
no more blown away by nature's forces

when morning comes the street sweepers arrive
a whirring roar storm's evidence removed
p g and e turns gadget power on
debris swept clean gale's evidence is gone

in the city

i woke up in the city
    its streets glistening from midnight rain
    its sirens sleeping after moonlit races
    and a street sweeper churning past padlocked bikes
    around a lone reveler stumbling from a nightclub past two

i woke up in the city
    to piercing alarms of bedside neighbors
    and pacing heels clicking to and fro
    on kitchen tiles and hardwood floors
    above my soot-stained window view

i woke up in the city
    confused at first by neon light
    with the early sun rising past the flickering glow
    and silver tower's shadow on townhomes row by row
    awash in white noise a streetcar passing through

i woke up in the city
    among unknown millions give or take
    in numbered streets and forgotten alleyways
    where wonders splendor worries magnificent
    blend in greys discarded among the unknown

*Original draft of "music for an abandoned warehouse"
written on the back of a concert program, May 20, 1990.*

music for an abandoned warehouse

a splattering of applause
and a low rumbling subway train
drift about a recovered warehouse alcove

hints of streetlight sneak through water-spotted panes
mixing with filtered stage light
and settling silent on paint-speckled floorboards

discordant jabs of sound fly from a frantic
swaying clarinet player's squeaking feet
that crisscross a boxy platform

a lonely photographer tiptoes
                              casting telltale shadows
his tripod carefully carried clunks
while pudgy fingers focus
                    click
the shutter shuts stage frozen in frame

a finale releases its echoey voice disappearing in plaster cracks
shifting floorboards
and a whirring reel of tape

two rows of battered buildings
stand silently outside
scarred by exhaust fumes flame and tagged by vandals
huddled close and cold
ignored by passing headlights

hidden behind tattered curtains four stories above the alcove
an elderly man holds his eyes to the stage
tempted by a trickle of music
squinting determined
following grimy distorted shadowy mimes
and patiently tasting his bottle of wine

from the window

dearborn station's clock approaches 2:15

    from the window

perspective rows of snow-stained brick
red and brown and weathered yellow
stretch back through infinite fog and shadow

    from the window

rooftop smoke scatters like startled pigeons
through trees naked and silent
lining the tired boulevard

    from the window

victorian dolls face inward
with crafted expressions and painted eyes
warmed by lavender-fringed petticoats

    from the window

listen carefully and
hear muted whispers of the city
distant sirens that race unseen sorrows

the green line

(now)

the green line trolley rumbles past park street | boylston | arlington
   | copley | hynes convention center | kenmore | fenway | longwood
   | brookline village | brookline hills | beaconsfield | reservoir
   | chestnut hill

each stop blurring one into another
a boston policeman sitting silent next to me
stiff cap pointed badge crisp jacket black boots eyes forward
my parents anxiously awaiting outside newton centre station

      i am eleven

(45 minutes ago)

i do what i always do locked in routine

"go down into the station
    put the fare in the fare box
        spin through the turnstile
           turn right / stairs down
               the tunnel beneath the tracks
                   connecting east to west and home"

the station quiet and empty
i turn to take the first step down
they surround me from the tunnel's shadows
ten boys maybe twelve buzzing with excitement

one pushes me and another and then
a hand clamps over my mouth
        (in that moment a memory burns:
        fingers rough on my lips
        sticky smell a sweaty palm
        a burst of terror
        unable to breath)

they pull me wrestling down the stairs
smothered mouth screams tears panic and then
in a moment
                a shout from across the tracks
                        they scatter into the shadows

the policeman must have appeared
or perhaps a ticket seller or passerby
i remember nothing and will never know
seconds minutes hours?
my mind erased by each stolen breath

and after a time sitting silent on the green line trolley

(50 minutes ago)

i do what I always do locked in routine

"go from mcdonald's to the park street station
        don't cross the street go into the station
                go down the stairs into the tunnel and under the tracks
                        that's how you go home"

my heart is still racing
when they reappear
ten boys maybe twelve laughing
surrounding me blocking the station entrance

"where are you going?"
    "leave me alone!" my shy voice trembling

again they disappear
so I step down

(60 minutes ago)

i do what i always do locked in routine

"after choir practice grab dinner next door
    at mcdonald's
        twenty should be plenty
            remember to bring home change!"

when turning from the counter
my tray full of dinner two boys approach
"are you alone?"
    "yes" my shy voice trembles
    (knowing "yes" is the wrong answer)

and then they are gone
leaving me alone
sweat tickling down my neck

(65 minutes ago)

i do what i always do locked in routine

"grab dinner before coming home
                mcdonald's is next door"

i walk out of the cathedral church of st. paul
steps away from boston's freedom trail
breathing in crisp fall air
choir practice hymns ringing in my ears

i am ready for dinner and the green line home

        it was wednesday

mixed tape

it's late after midnight flipping through vinyl
punk – new wave – ska – industrial – goth
tilting albums on edge like bookmarks in the stacks
my jet-black hair a teased homage to robert smith

what songs will make you smile?
   moisten your eyes?
      spark a memory?
         move you to dance?
            calm your racing mind until you sleep?

sliding each album from its sleeve
balanced on edge
                        feeling for the spindle
i drop the needle while cueing the tape

side one: songs for dance

depeche mode master and servant the cure lovecats new order blue monday
each song chosen to tingle your nerves until they overload
i imagine you mouthing the words
                                    headphones snug
twirling across your kitchen floor

side two: songs for escape

cocteau twins oomingmak björk isobel eurythmics this city never sleeps
each song chosen to float waves of bliss a soothing melancholy tide
instead of dancing I imagine you lying back

                                       eyes closed
disappearing into the pulsing bass

and later
i imagine you reading the liner notes
on the cardboard sleeve slipped inside
you smiling

            thinking of me
flipping the tape
to press play again

or perhaps
you'll leave the tape in your civic

                        forgotten
until discovered years later by a passenger's rummaging
and feeling the beat of the first song

                            you'll discreetly wipe a tear

three

i leave behind cool sheets for shadows
mawu's tendrils tease me through
past stovepipes puffing tufts of memories
through wispy cumulus mist in blue

carved

1

the sculptor prepares her tools
a discarded dentist probe for subtle detail
a twisted rake and wire brush to drape skin

stepping back
she searches inside the polymer clay block
for figures hidden awaiting release

she starts by sculpting with her fingers
digging smoothing molding the clay
until features emerge

one tool then another
shaping carving blending occasionally placing slabs of clay
to form curled hair or add a flowing skirt

the sculptor's world collapses inward city cacophony muted
just fingers tools clay working
until in time there is nothing left to carve

2

the poet prepares his tools
a blank page for letters syllables words phrases
a puzzle to untangle finding order and place

stepping back he stares at the empty page
searching memories for images
to transform into well-ordered lines

he starts with random words
pleasing sounds rhymes and throwaway couplets
to be worked and reworked

words become phrases become stanzas
whispered aloud to test their resonance set aside to revisit later
discarded when impossible to mold

the poet searches for perfection
pacing the floor perplexed
until with a final pen stroke the poem appears

3

the sculptor's work set on a shelf
the poet's page slipped in a book
visions carved in clay and words
buried deep unseen unheard

in the overnight

in the overnight resisting ripples
of sleep staring down on twinkling street lights
by towering cities clusters of homes
smudged translucent by feathery vapor

wing tip winks through my window seat portal
a steady metallic heartbeat tick tock
the tiny red glow reflects in thin air
gliding so graceful suspended in sky

perhaps down below sleepless and staring
winking wing tip taps through clouds distorted
a wispy aura painted on cirrus
engines' roar muted swallowed in darkness

soon city lights give way to lifeless grey
a blackout veil separates land from air
flight path hidden no beginning no end
up down forward back all rolled into one

darkness decays into morning's return
dawn peeks over the distant horizon
in the overnight soaring and silent
high above the promise of tomorrow

mawu after midnight

the velvet black of after midnight
darkness rich in new moon's blur
siren singsong distant wailing
steady hummm mechanical whir

i leave behind cool sheets for shadows
mawu's tendrils tease me through
past stovepipes puffing tufts of memories
through wispy cumulus mist in blue

nocturnal sprites show off their dances
sky cast grey its color spent
dreamscape dunes form in the distance
ochre smoothed by sandstorm's vent

new moon hints but ever hidden
star points' constellation spine
galactic dust distant tucana
comets etch a glittering line

further out near big bang's edge
where her secrets safely kept
upon a throne of glistening carbon
songs in whispers softly wept

in darkness pure expanding outwards
trace her outline forward and back
time spun and twirled in escher's loop
mawu's silhouette sketched in black

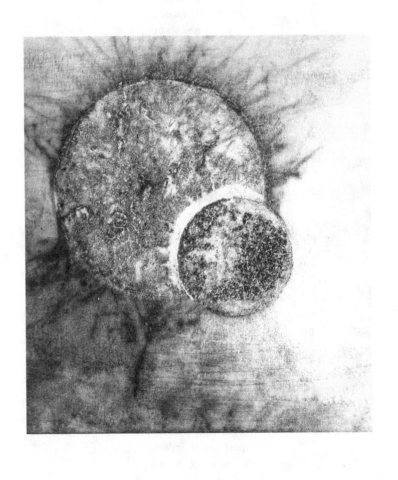

wade

echoes
om tibetan
singing bowls
resonating humm
by cool water seeping
through ancient crevices
building to flow over creek
beds lined with time smoothed
pebbles wading deeper in darkness
leaving an invisible wake while
my fingers follow fractured
barren blackened shale
consuming all light
the ageless crush
buried stone
haunted
depth

earth
slips away
weightless toes
free legs torso float
soaring above
infinity's
edge

wading
thru sunlit
dancing water
sparkling in indigo
swaying waist-deep toe
tips grip tide-shaped sand
white cap topped waves
bahamian sun swirls
arms outstretched
fingers reach
balance

jolted
shoulder taps
you nodded off time
for bed shuffling through
nighttime nuisances one by one
so i can wade back into sleep
to search for bahamian
surf or the depths of
buried stone

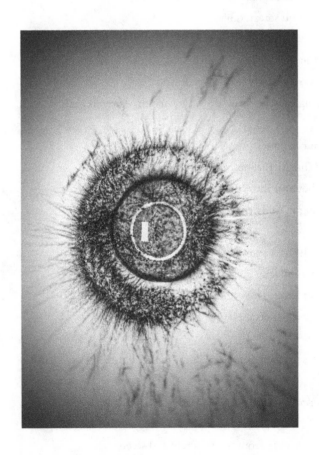

etchings

i start writing perched waist-deep on a bahamian sand bar
tracing letters in azure-blue surf
the letters momentary wisps on an endless swelling tide

letters words trace back to shore
rising tide chases sand-traced stanzas
leaving behind smeared blurs

chasing the tide i take my words away from waves' encroach
writing more quickly now more furious
challenging each crashing wave to catch my lettered trails

my poem continues from surf to sand clouds
chopped fine by turboprop turns
tracing thoughts into cool vapor mist
left floating in midair

my poem lies dormant now
chilled by mundane grey and skyline smog
i try to cut letters from the soot and smoke
only to see them crumble like ash

evelyn sees me grabs my hand cleaning away the dust and grime

   daddy daddy! follow me i know where you can write!

she leads me away from the concrete and steel
to a small city park a sandbox nestled
in trees that let sunlight through the blanket of grey

daddy try this!

she hands me a freshly fallen branch

i write in the sand circling around us
until entrapped my daughter claps and twirls

the poem ends briskly at sunset
when cold shivers come from the pacific shore
strolling lovers pause by the sand-etched stanzas
as they are slowly whisked away by a moonlit winter breeze

ricochets

sometimes
among restless dreams
rain creeps in
a slow percussive blend
of ricochets
carelessly dangling over tiles
into troughs
and coupled spouts
gathering in pools
slick on moonlit pavement

pulling
        catching
                a discarded note

its message dissolved into swirling texture

streams drink more streams
with runoffs swift
(soon raging)
snaking to pacific's bay
led by moon-pulled tides

when the deluge slows
and ricochets soften to
steady drips
and the moon peeks out
to shoo away puddles
will sleep follow?

or will i lie awake listening
for hints of her return?

north south east west

from the north

a pungent scent of vineyard fields
cabernet blended with cherry plum currant
and wisps from an unkempt campfire ember
or power-line arc or echoed boom of dry lightning

from the south

tendrils of brown reach into california's blue sky
flames racing through well-worn trails
chasing cougars into farmers' fields
sending suburbanites scurrying for filtered air

from the east

north and south now swirling into one
blazing vineyard fields and engulfed redwoods
while cal fire air tankers soar into the torrent
above a line of red trucks and their smoke-hardened fighters

from the west

brisk pacific breeze nudges smoke into valleys
leaving a clear cool salt-scented wake
barefoot toes drinking the tide
and for a moment forgetting

and then it was still

winds settle north south east and west
moon's rays refracted through remanent smoke
distant fires regroup awaiting tomorrow
windows long closed now open a little

reach

reach and unfurl smooth tendrils of silver thread
set them down in perfect parallel lines
set them just so a breath apart
one by one by one
until silver lines blur into shades of grey
shining smooth and sterile into the horizon

reach and dig out pebbles worn smooth by ocean surf
set them down still damp and glistening
set them just so a breath apart
geometric swirls opening ever outward
until they make shadows drawn by sunset's glow

reach inside for buried fears
precisely set a breath apart
each in metered rhyming rows
calligraphed and jet black dark

reach down and take my trembling hand
guide me to horizon's edge
fears now set upon the page
until the ink begins to fade

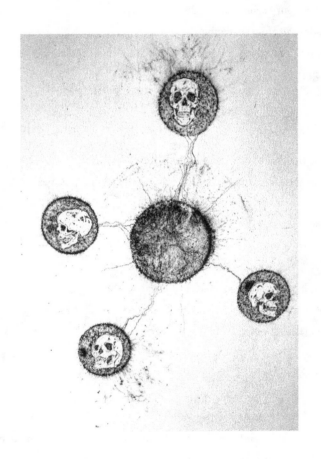

silence too

you ask me for silence

so i tug on your earbuds and hide them away
music fades but in its place the city rumbles
a cacophony of impatient honks and speeding sirens and rubber squealing
across asphalt

i need more you say!

so i pause the traffic but in its place the sidewalk hums
a click clack click of hurried heels and pair of yapping poodles and
neighbors' voices rising

more more more you say!

so i send them on their way but in their place tilt up to the sky
a distant roar of jet contrails and circling copter's pulsing flutter and rustle of
a squirrel leaping between hickory-oak branches

i still need more you plead!

so i clear the skies and shoo the squirrel but in its place the ocean awakes
clamoring seagulls on trade wind swells and surf crashing and the delicate
crickle of a fire pit carved in sand

more you plead just a little more!

so i nudge the surf into the ocean depths but in its place your house begins
to speak

creaks from aging floorboards and tickling mice behind your walls and the plip plop of your daughter's feet

is there still more you whisper?

so i send your daughter to bed and brush your eyelids still but in their place new sounds emerge tingling tinnitus that never fades and rustling fingers between the sheets and the poom poom in your chest

breathe i whisper back so softly you can barely hear me

just breathe until in sleep your questions cease

powder

fingertips stained by
pistol powder piled
burying brush strokes

you twist the fuse wires
tucking them snug
awaiting battery's spark

when you ignite the powder
time distorts
a blinding flash
of flame and smoke
a metal tube
focussing flying detritus
from chain reaction's fury

when fire cools
steam drifts away
scorched canvas revealed
you delicately carve
the soot-soaked clay
unveiling a tattered flag

transfixed
by blackened brush strokes
delicate lines and flame
i savor the lingering scent
of scorched powder

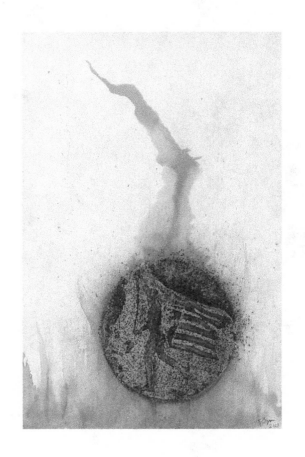

four

beneath the church bells you may find
cool water running clean
out from a spout of aging brass
a liquid cool serene

sounds of vienna

clip clop clip clop
    horse's hoofs start and stop
the driver's click to make them go
    carriage wheels gild just for show

dingle-dring dingle-dring
    vienna's cyclists a speedy thing
step quick aside as they zip by
    a whoosh of air blink of an eye

rumble and hum rumble and hum
    the trolley car wheels announce as they come
doors open quick get in get out
    then to the next platz before turning about

drubble-dee drubble drubble-dee drubble
    those damn cobblestones are a whole lot of trouble
the heel of her shoe may catch on a crack
    causing a trip fall down with a smack

clang and dong clang and dong
    stephansdom bells are starting a song
parishioners called from far and from wide
    cool pews in shadows a nice place to hide

birdsong's peal birdsong's peal
    the morning's come it's sunlight i feel
our vienna trip's over to venice we go
    what sound does a gondola make do you know?

tunnels

dark to light | light to dark
alpine ranges sheer cliffs stark

arches appear thirty meters per second
strobe-lit tunnels echoes that beckon

in my rearview mirror evening sun fades
around the next corner there's shadow and shade

summit and valley | tunnel and span
asphalt trails impassive and planned

infinite vista trapped behind glass
i focus on lanes and the traffic we pass

i long for an unbeaten trail to explore
random adventures through a once-hidden door

until then i drive between parallel lines
imagining journeys beyond exit signs

5 abbey road

let it be and maxwell's hammer
    (whistle passersby)

speeding taxis honking lorries
    (buzzing mopeds fly)

fans dart out in twos and fours
    (stagger-stepped in space)

while friends frame up click and run
    (the traffic held in place)

a simple zebra crossing drawn
    (on abbey road near 5)

a place where all you need is love
    (the fab four dreams alive)

limano

a wooden door abandoned
for a horse barn built of stone
a courtyard set with wildflowers
sitting all alone

an aging calico creeps by
pursuing phantom mice
the baker's wife throws open shutters
fills the air with spice

connected stone a wall of bricks
create the mountain roads
carved from apuane ridges
for mule carts' heavy loads

the roads lead up from serchio's bed
(where perfect stones are found)
stones that rolled from higher places
resting on wet ground

beneath the church bells you may find
cool water running clean
out from a spout of aging brass
a liquid cool serene

tucked behind a soaring tower
walls from granite born
tunneled arches sun and shadow
cool breeze in the 'morn

awake with hints of batter mixed
from ground chestnut flour
necci cooked on ferri plates
for the lunchtime hour

the only sound for careful ears
that search the mountain air
a distant peal a child's laughter
from a traveling fair

sandcastles in the snow

we made sandcastles in the snow
    abetone crystals mixed with lido's sun-burnt sand
    dissolving into cool steam from mountain ice

we made sandcastles in the snow
    behind us lines of parasols sand raked clean in even rows
    north africans with goods in tow shivering in alpine breeze

we made sandcastles in the snow
    our knees salt-stained and glazed with sand
    our fingers tingling through frozen sheets

we made sandcastles in the snow
    dreaming of ocean glass in still mountain air
    as far beyond horizon's edge tomorrow awaits

five towers

a dizzying twirl to stefansdom's peak
steps block on block hug a solitary column
far below nestled in the catacombs keep
eleven thousand souls sleep in silence
crypts burrowed deep in dirt and rubble
bones skulls stacked in even rows
saints sinners plague victims unknown

south from stefandom's patterned tiles
past venezian canals and gondolier splendor
over hillsides vineyards mediterranean shores
leans pisa's torre pendente
stone steps circle a slanted hollow core
worn uneven by i turisti swaying to and fro
far below lovers support the tower in framed relief

free from pisa's peak over chianti vigne and san gimignano gates
fly sienese flags — seventeen contrade unfurled for il palio's race
in centuries unchanged these medieval dreams
under piazza del campo's slender tower
where narrow crouching darkness leads to clear bells' call
and duomo's colored stone silhouettes in prayer

chianti grapes and tuscan hills lead to apuane ridges
stadtturm — innsbruck's city tower — encased in dolomite ice and stone
stark severe graceful majestic ancient peaks
look down and gaze at steps of modern steel and ancient oak
a platform open air where bells now silent once tolled
and pastel apartments lined up side by side in cool dusk's breeze

calling their children home

salzach's waters swelled by winter's melting drifts
hohensalzburg's keep overlooks
cobblestone streets give way to funicular rails
rising to a solitary peak
where gazing out brings shivers in the hot june sun
turrets of white topaz domes and slender points of gild
from stone-carved steps to open air eyes closed a trumpet sounds
a single note propelled above five towers lost in echoes

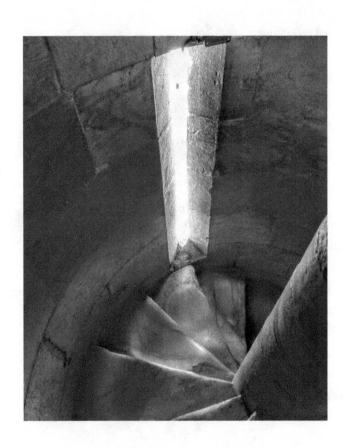

arcata community forest

shirtless bearded hippies sail
    (by gravity's pull down the trail)
sky-high pupils a hazed hello
    (scented wakes that wave below)

around a turn lush valleys fall
    (in swansong fog and redwoods tall)
while high above aged sequoias groan
    (and down below roots squeeze the loam)

a knife-carved bench overlooks hooved passes
    (distracted horses refuge in stray grasses)
hollowed stumps house midnight flames
    (while younger trunks twirl playful games)

i climb these circles drawn in carta
    (a treasured oasis steps from eureka)
when backdrop soothes night sounds begin
    (the last drop drained to home again)

my eyes closed still where the trail begins

serpents

driving back from reno
up a twisting mountain pass
either side lie serpents
as i silently trespass

|

rotting posts standing close
tilted buried shallow
crooked serpent silent
traverses fields left fallow

|

bolted rail ties anchored tight
make a wooden spine
elegantly engineered
in parallel steel lines

|

this serpent stretches on for miles
making graceful traces
racing forward never touching
into distant places

|

i pass a serpent churning soil
mixed with suntanned silt
fields with lines of towering stalks
hiding hints of gilt

|

nearby sandbags line a river
making curvy walls
ready to hold back flood's fury
when the first drop falls

|

bemused by these impostors
still under wind smoothed stone
this serpent lies forgotten
now silent all alone

|

its tongue ever tasting air
awaiting passing prey
masked by swirling dancing sand
that paints the air in grey

The next six poems are sequences from a long poem, *portraits of red and grey (russia 1983 no gorby perestroika or hint of democracy)*. The poems recount a high school trip to the USSR that spanned eighteen remarkable days, with barely a day or two in each city. It was an unforgettable experience I wrote about years later as a term project for a creative writing course while attending The University of Waterloo.

portraits of red and grey #3

our pilot attacks heaven without mercy
racing for altitude
an ear-popping ascent ripping through clouds
i grip my seat
i am used to north american comfort

relief
the plane levels
cruising softly
        brushing cloud tops

waiting
    waiting
      waiting

        at the last possible moment to land
        dive-bombing the runway
        like a kamikaze dropping
        popping my ears confused vertical vertigo

gripping the ground
relieved
russian arms to inspect me
        armed and stone-faced

a young soldier in a box
his eyes passing back
        and forth
from my passport to me

saying nothing

          signaling another young soldier

their eyes through me

i try to stare back

i try not to sweat

portraits of red and grey #6

vodka party!

stolichnaya
bottles in every hand

> (pepper vodka
> lemon vodka)

drink after drink after...

it's my first-ever drink
i'm not sure what to do

> how much to swallow

it feels burning hot

> then fuzzy

(tastes horrible)

i feel my way along walls towards the bathroom
spinning
slumping

> (a loud shout? somewhere? knocking?)

back into marshie's room
crumbling into a corner
maybe it's late

later

i find my room door key fumbling fall
phil's in the can

> (for hours)

i'm banging on the door
he won't come out

pissing in a pop bottle
careful aim in desperation

flopping onto
                    i hope
a bed

falling into a pitch-black spiral
passing out

out

portraits of red and grey #7

a suspensionless bus
will not let me forget
last night's vodka party

moscow passes blurred
famous churches statues buildings museums

                       (i can't remember)

until the shades of grey reveal

red square

i walk on stones rich in history
my breath sucked out in open space

                       (walls towering
                           enclosing
                           silent)

a tv image explodes before me

                    peter jennings
                    live
                    from
                    moscow

i cannot see i cannot hear
the parades of missiles
or cries of revolution

              but i feel them
              beneath my feet

portraits of red and grey #8

we are lined up
silent respectful

        fearful

lenin's tomb before us
hundreds ahead in line
good citizens on their yearly pilgrimage

glazed guards stifle our approach
a tomb of simple shining marble (a bunker)
a single entrance
poised bayonets line our path

        we keep our hands at our sides
        walk slowly
        breathe silently

someone ahead scratches an ear
sharpened blades level from all sides

        shouts in russian

the line stops waits and
continues

    (false alarm)
i check my hands

gripping my pants

steps inside a downward spiral
a bulletproof-glass–encased shoe

                                        leg
                                        waist
                                        chest
                                        head

peculiar
            preserved
                        waxy
                                    unreal

portraits of red and grey #15

sipping tea in samarkand
a nestled perch
on concrete stilts
an eerie cove
in shadows glow
from sunlight seeping
patterned walls
open air a warmer breeze
so strangely whispers
this hidden space
on kneeling mats and
wooden slats
a simple teacup held in place

portraits of red and grey #16

we run into green foothills
like the von trapp family
the mountains before us
a wall hiding warring afghanistan
    (50 miles by crow flight)
dushanbe lit glorious
warmth springing from sunlight
summer bursting outwards
fierce from its slumber

we run and gasp through thinning air
tiring quickly
               breathing sharply
a simple picnic
eaten on boulders
watching the snow line
melt beneath our feet

revived we slide in slush and mud
skiing in sneakers
               carving trails in liquid grass
we glide towards a small village
hidden in a valley
ignoring our impatient bus driver's calls

the village's houses are frail

                    precarious

thin sheet metal roofs

               barely balanced

      teeter

a naked man stands oblivious

  in a shower without walls

chickens peck at our footprints

  funny and furious

a statue of lenin (hollow plastic)

                        as small as the village

                        bolted stronger than rooftops

stands proud and defiant

on a slab of grey concrete

five

i saw beauty resting in dimming light
your head held still on a slender palm
stories told with moistened lips slight and shimmering
i could only listen

tethered

i've long ago learned to ignore
the rhythmic tug of the chain
that tethers me to the ocean floor

a chill curls around my painted stripes
as fog rolls toward a distant shore
and wave-powered bells warn those sailing near

i hear passing ships cutting towards
the golden gate and imagine their
carefully stacked containers swaying in the swells

later fog fades and california's sun
steams dew from my metallic frame
unveiling the shore's outline once more

a seagull pauses perched and
chattering singing me stories until
trade winds lift her to dance above white caps

soon the season of storms returns
bringing fierce waves and wind
to power the peals of my warning bells

deep in winter mist freezes
to my metallic skin crafting
turquoise crystals that flicker in the moonlight

but in time calm and warmth return
lit by the moon's waning crescent
mirrored on still water's glass

do i measure time in seasons? or in dawns and dusks?
or count the cycles of frost freezing
then dripping melted down my spine?

or do i set aside time and count the swells?
or passing ships? or pods of dolphins
shivers of sharks colonies of gulls?

i dream of one day being released from my tether
my work complete transformed into turquoise sea glass
smoothed by tides and resting on a shoreline beach
waiting to catch the eye of a strolling passerby

waiting for sunrise

for Mary on the day of our wedding

the sun will speak in whispers today
of magic and dreams and beauty
splinters of light will draw us forward
to a meeting place high above feathery clouds
the same golden bands that bring us together
wait to unite us for a magical journey

it is early still as i wait for sunrise
patient and calm in still summer's darkness
i close my eyes and feel that gold
your slender hand in mine
our souls swirling weightless
a dream that escaped the prison of sleep
floats alive to meet the rising dawn

140 characters

0123456789012345678901234567890123456789012345678901234567890123456789890123456789012345678901234
5678901234567890123456789012345678901234567890123456789012345678901234567890123456789
0123456789

only one hundred and forty characters left to share a pacific
ocean fog that whistles and swirls around me like chilled
hands seeking warmth

a few more characters and later in darkness i'll wrap my
fingers and senses around your distant skin untouched by
winter's cavernous embrace

and maybe with a message tapped i can pause your heart from
its rushing to and fro and in that moment with only words
steal your breath away

with each thought sent i wonder as the characters disappear
silently into the sky from my hand to yours if they playfully
change their shape

do the characters shift and twirl turning words and phrases
into carelessly typed meaningless jumbles? or do they stay
locked in rigid lines

and laugh or weep or sigh from the messages they form? or
do they lie awake trembling unable to forget their part in
a final anguished plea?

i can't believe that these characters are nothing more than
fleeting digital beats: easily swiped away or left unanswered
in a digital stack

yet in the silence awaiting your reply i wonder whether my
message strayed, hid deep inside the white noise floating
between us in the night

brush strokes and flickering shadows

in memory of sheryl noonan

down below tiptoe with care into the room where shadows grow
    where cocooned nestled draped and still the filmstrip rests by furnace glow

a garden strung of hanging cels pictures reversed so cool and slight
    her captured frames my shoulders brush their stories sing in fading light

the first cel taken by cupid's true arrow
    a smooth sculptured sprite in silvery gold
the artist's slight frame eyes focused and narrow
    brush and palette grasped a well-postured hold

cels flicker back softly two sisters in pose
    curled fingers together in loving embrace
a pair of young sculptors on winnipeg snow
    wrapped in crystals and fur on white sheets of lace

or a moment suspended the swing at its arc
    our smiles so joyful in that sun-captured frame
my face seems to tell her again! higher! faster!
    these memories timeless undated unnamed

the next cel a view of manhattan's famed skyline
    an unfinished beauty the canvas wood grain
feathered strokes inspired by nature's work guided
    pencil sketch shadows ever waiting for stain

a rough rush of air as the subway car passes
    the crowd pushes forward i glance was it you?
and forward i'm pressed with the ttc masses
    then years trickle by that slight sighting now through

in a room crossed and guarded protectors still waiting
    i flip through the cels ever searching for reason
every corner stacked perfect for balanced detection
    i cry for your terror this delusional prison

are feared shadows now scattered by infinite light
    no longer trapped in celluloid frames?
i dream your art soars now free of the night
    peace be with you dear sherry ever more ever slight

beauty

for Mary

i saw beauty beyond a towering cumulus top
storming over verdant hills caressed by passing gales
and an emerald figure vanishing

i could only watch

i saw beauty resting in dimming light
your head held still on a slender palm
stories told with moistened lips slight and shimmering

i could only listen

i saw beauty in sleep like death
so calm yet breathing still
tucked out of sight in twilight's shadow

i could only feel

i saw beauty deep inside your pupils' ochre rings
passion cloaked by solitude unyielding
rainbow shades i can see but never touch
dreams that awaken me drenched but i cannot recall
and a whisper in the air so sweet infectious pure
that i search the earth's crevasses for just one breath

i saw beauty and it was you

ode to sabby

before a final breath you shivered soft
i stroked your fur and shed a silent tear
this kitten once now rests so still and frail
and in that moment closed your final year

travel back the day when we first met
a condo hall where you would run and play
we'd set you loose your tiny paws would fly
up and down as long as we would stay

back at school you joined me in my dorm
to scamper while i studied late at night
you'd wait to pounce until i'd least suspect
and on my shoulder land a phantom sprite

together we drove down the 401
tercel packed full with clothes and vinyl crates
you purred and stretched toronto in our sights
while waterloo behind in distance fades

you waited when we married years ago
likely asleep as vows and rings exchanged
our family began with just us three
with everything in place so well arranged

our honeymoon delayed a mortgage closed
you enter our first house with sniffs explore
and search from room to room to find your place
a patch of rug in sunshine on the floor

each christmas you would hide beneath the tree
and wait until all decorating done
with stealth we'd watch you sneak up from below
and with your paw knock loose the closest one

when babies came you sniffed them cautiously
so patient when their small hands tugged your fur
and as they grew you were their faithful friend
to calm their fears with cuddles and a purr

until one day your frame so slight and frail
we knew the time had come to say goodbye
i carried you one last time in my arms
and held you as a doctor helped you die

epilogue

This collection ends with poems I wrote as a teenager nearly forty years ago. I edited, typed (on an IBM Selectric typewriter), designed (cut and glued), printed, assembled, and distributed these poems as part of a student collection titled *Viewless Wings*. I remember the positive feedback from fellow high school students who connected with the poetry created by their peers. *Viewless Wings* paid tribute to this poem by Keats:

> *Away! away! for I will fly to thee,*
> *Not charioted by Bacchus and his pards,*
> *But on the viewless wings of Poesy*

From "Ode to a Nightingale" by John Keats

silk suspenders

take me away
far away
to a city in the clouds
suspended by silk threads
swaying in a cool breeze

leave me by the front gate
on the north side
i'll wander through tranquil gardens
forever stopping to probe rich air filled with the yellowpurplelavender
of a thousand flowers

later
when soft shadows begin to grow
i'll walk down cobblestone lanes
unmarred by carriage wheels
past marble shops
with lace-curtained windows

                                    a pet store
with laughing collies
inviting

               chocolate
from the bakery next door
a warm thick scent
holding me in temptation

and whenever i feel dull
or bored
i'll use my sharpened razor

to cut another silk thread
and feel the city shiver
beneath my feet

formality

spent
all my
money
on dinner
and a corsage
for my
beautiful
date
and for cocktails
and a limousine
and for a
tuxedo
with red lines
down the
legs
and on tickets
and on mix
for the
party
and found out
she is a
vegetarian
as the steaks arrived
and
discovered she gets
carsick
easily when drinking

and uncovered her
dislike
for dancing
and painfully acknowledged
her curfew
as i spent
all my change
on
a taxi
to take her
home

pony ride in the sky

pony ride in the sky
with daddy holding the reins
                              out front
and me on top
keeping one-eyed teddy
close to the steaming thick-haired body

we sail light-headed through airless space
the beaten dirt path
                        forgotten
below

"daddy
        don't go too high
 mommy might see us
                and worry"

and falling back to earth
whistling through red-brown autumn treetops
a cascade of broken branches
follows us
           down

overture to silence

stop for a second
sit on your urban sofa
see if you can find
                    silence
switch off your tv   and washer
                    and radio   and dryer

send your kids away
give your wife the eaton's card

turn off your central heating's hsssss

close all your windows
                    and doors

cut your power and water
disconnect fluorescent hummm

go deep in your basement

        and wait

        patiently

        until

        there are no sirens
                    or barking dogs

and wait until you can only hear
that spider walking across your arm
carefully squeeze
                    hold your breath
silence

Acknowledgements

Despite writing poetry for almost forty years, tackling the challenge of publishing a book was sparked by three simple words from a good friend. In late 2020 Kari Byron (host of *MythBusters* and *Crash Test World* and author of *Crash Test Girl*), texted me, "Write more poetry." That encouragement, and a year of pandemic-induced creativity, gave me the confidence to craft a book from my portfolio of poems. Kari's extraordinary black-powder painting *We the People* inspired the poem "powder."

My wife Mary and my father played key roles as editors. My wife provided unflinchingly honest and *actionable* feedback. My father Philip Morehead (a published author from the Morehead family tree of authors) provided an extra layer of keen insights. Combined they pushed me to work through many poetic puzzles. I also want to thank the network of friends and colleagues who have been moved by the poems I've written over the years and helped convince me that writing a book wasn't a vanity project.

Finally I want to thank the high school English teachers who encouraged my love of poetry, in particular Wayne Tompkins, my grade ten creative writing teacher, as well as Terence Bredin, Marshall Webb, and Ross Morrow. Collectively they played a key role in my love of writing.

JAMES MOREHEAD is a product manager by day, poet by night. "canvas" is his debut collection. While attending the University of Waterloo for Computer Engineering he took every English course he could fit into his schedule. He calls both the USA and Canada home, and is currently based in the San Francisco Bay Area.

viewlesswingspress.com | Twitter: @dublinranch
Instagram: @viewlesswings | LinkedIn: linkedin.com/in/morehead/